10-12-15 Water damage noted. WS

Going to the Potty

Going to the Potty

BY FRED ROGERS

photographs by Jim Judkis

Penguin Putnam Books for Young Readers

With special thanks to: Nan Earl Newell, Research;
Margaret B. McFarland, Ph.D., Senior Consultant; Barry N. Head;
the Newell family; the Robinson family and the other parents
and children who agreed to help us with the book.

Printed on recycled paper

A PaperStar Book, published in 1997 by Penguin Putnam Books for Young Readers,
345 Hudson Street, New York, NY 10014. PaperStar Books is a registered trademark of
The Putnam Berkley Group, Inc. The PaperStar logo is a trademark of The Putnam Berkley
Group, Inc. Originally published in 1986 by G. P. Putnam's Sons.
Published simultaneously in Canada. Printed in the United States of America.
Library of Congress Cataloging-in-Publication Data
Rogers, Fred. Going to the potty. (A Mister Rogers' First experience book)
SUMMARY: Parent and child may read together about the way children develop in the experience
of eliminating waste products from their body and about the positive aspect of using the toilet.
1. Children—Hospital care—Juvenile literature.
{1. Toilet training.}   I. Judkis, Jim, ill.   II. Title.   III. Series: Rogers, Fred.
Mister Rogers' First experience book.   HQ 7705.R64   1986   649'.62   85-24410
ISBN 0-698-11575-9
10   9   8

Learning to take charge of body functions may not be an easy task for a young child, but it is as natural and inevitable as learning to use a spoon or to tie a shoe. Nevertheless, few aspects of a child's development arouse greater concern among parents or invite more conflict between parent and child than what we call toilet training.

It seems to me that the "training" that happens in toilet training is really a joint effort. We parents train our children in the mechanics of the process, but we also learn how to respond to cues of our children's *readiness* to be trained. Only when a child has a certain measure of mental awareness and muscular control can training ever begin to be successful.

It's sometimes hard for parents not to measure a child's success by what the books say or by the standards of another sibling or a friend's child. But for each child, the timetable for learning to use the potty is as individual as learning to walk or talk. Expecting too much too soon can lead to frustration for both parents and children.

When we parents have realistic expectations about the toilet training process, we are more likely to approach it with a comfortable balance of gentleness and persistence. And our children are more likely to gain from the experience not just mastery of their body functions, but a stronger sense of self . . . of the unique human beings they really are becoming. Toilet training for parents and children is another way of saying "I love you."

—Fred Rogers

NOTE: Throughout this book I have used adult terminology for body functions. As you read this with your child, you may be more comfortable substituting the words with which your own family is familiar.

When babies are little, there are many things they can't do by themselves.

They can't get dressed by themselves.

They can't even eat by themselves.
There are *lots* of things their moms
and dads need to do for them!

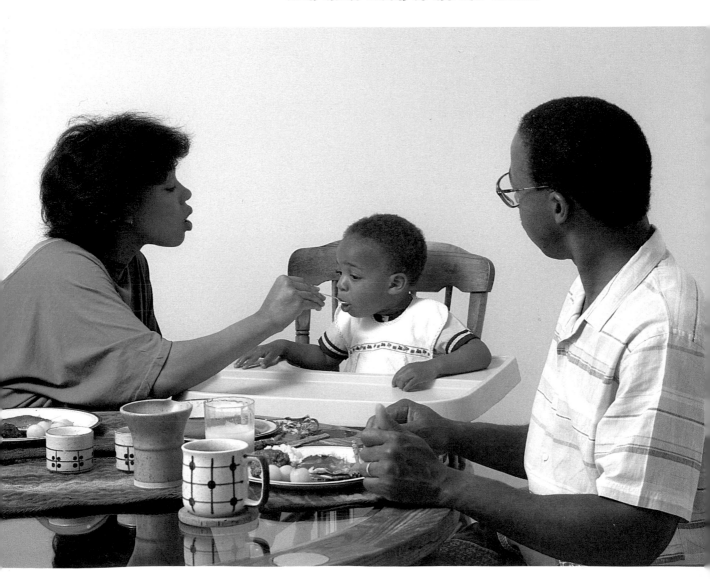

Babies wear diapers. Some
diapers are made of cloth,
and some are made of paper
and plastic. Sometimes
they feel warm and dry.

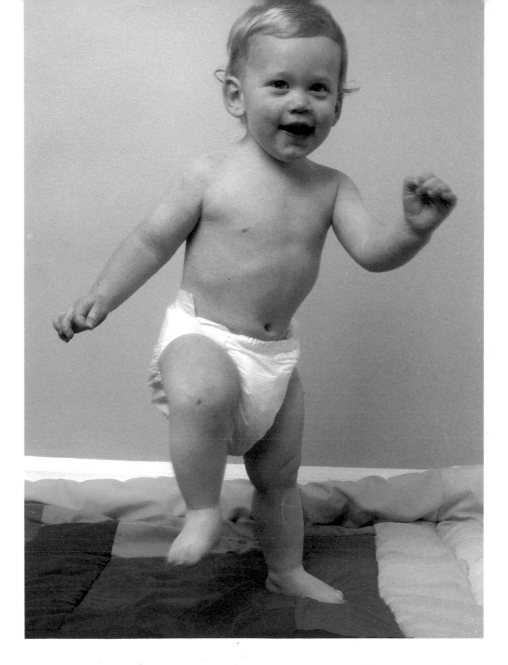

If you wear diapers, you know how good that can feel.

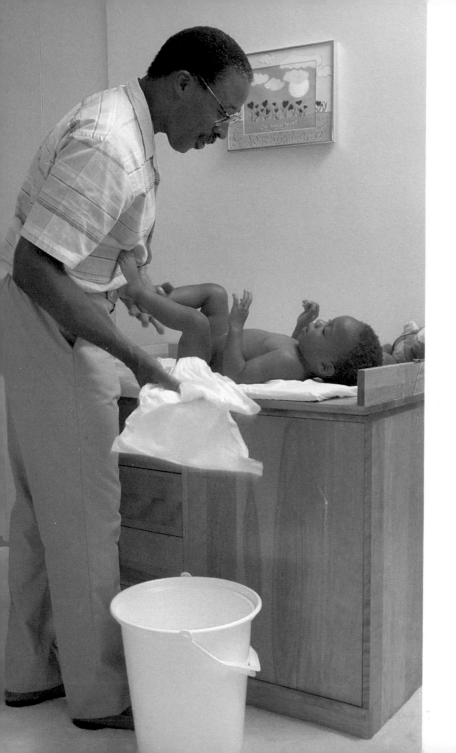

But sometimes diapers
get wet and messy and
have to be changed.
Paper diapers get
thrown away,

. . . but cloth diapers get washed and used again. Changing diapers is another way moms and dads take care of their children.

When babies grow older, they begin to do lots of things by themselves. They learn how to feed themselves and how to wash and get dressed.

They learn new ways to play, too. Sometimes they like to make pictures with crayons or with their hands.

Sometimes they like to play in special places with water
or sand. Are you learning to do some of these things?

Something else children learn as they grow is how to urinate and make bowel movements (BMs) in the toilet instead of their diapers. Urine and BMs come out of our bodies. They're things our bodies don't need.

Do you have special names for them? It can take a long time for children to feel ready to use a toilet just the way older children and grown-ups do!

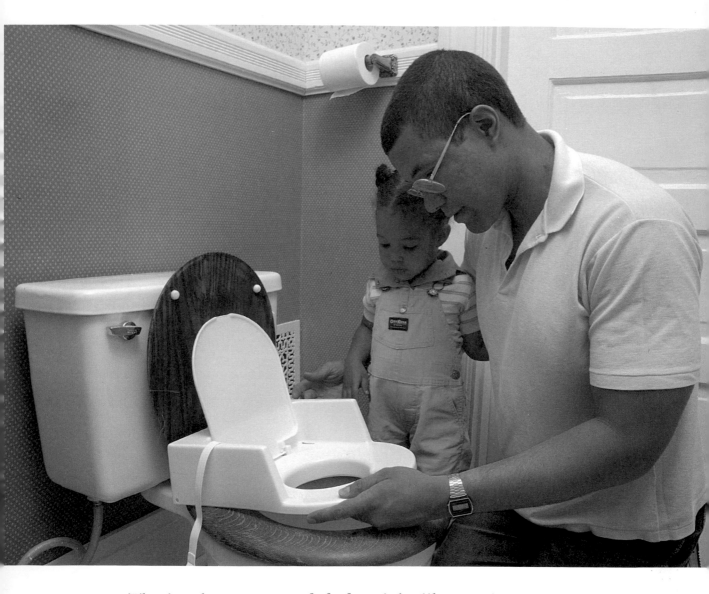

That's why moms and dads might like to give
them a special kind of chair to begin with.
It could be a seat that fits on the toilet.

Or it could be a potty-chair that sits on the floor and has a little pot underneath. Do you have a chair or seat like that? Some children like to sit right on the toilet seat. But others feel better sitting on something that lets their feet touch the floor.

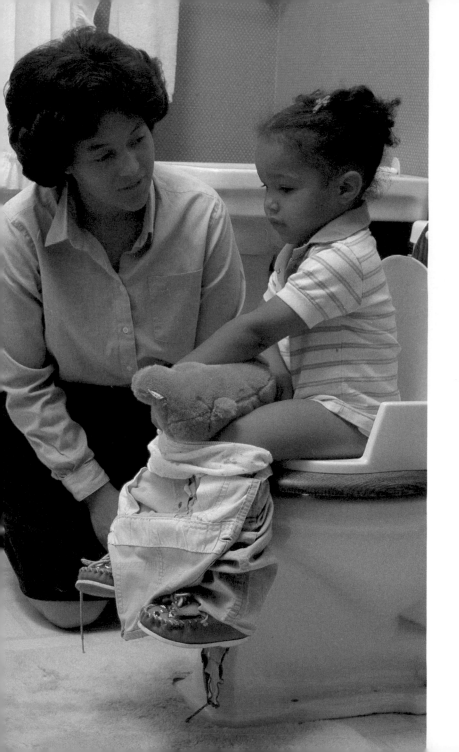

It can take a while
to get used to sitting
on one of these special
seats. At first it may feel
a little hard and cold.

That only lasts for a few moments, though, and then it feels fine.

When you feel ready, you may be able to urinate and make BMs in the pot under the potty-chair or right in the toilet. Children need to take their time about things like that.

Girls and women
sit down to urinate
and make BMs.

Boys and men often stand
up when they urinate. But
they always sit down when
they make BMs, too.

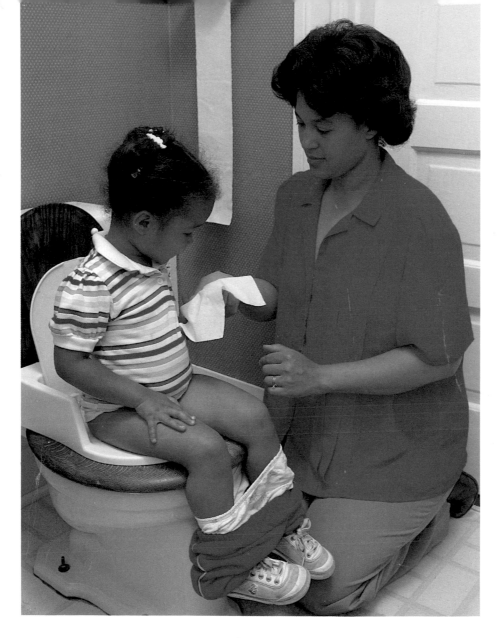

Learning to wipe yourself clean can be hard at first.
Often moms and dads have to help with that for a while.

Have you ever watched a toilet flush? All that water can make a lot of noise. Toilets are meant to flush away *only* things we don't need.

When you first start
trying to go to the
potty, you may find
it hard to get there
on time.

Some children wet or mess in their pants now and
then before they really get used to going to the potty.

Learning to stay
clean and dry is
one way to please
your mom and dad
and you!

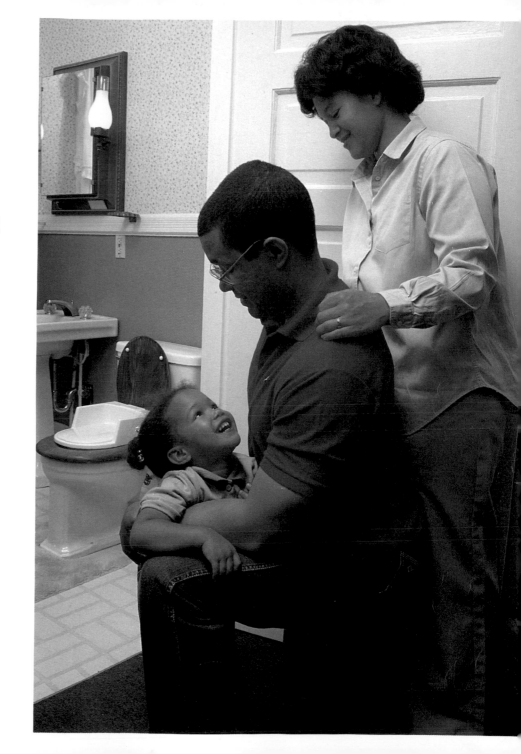

If you ever need to go to
the potty when you're away
from home, you can always
ask the adults with you to
help you find a bathroom
you can use.

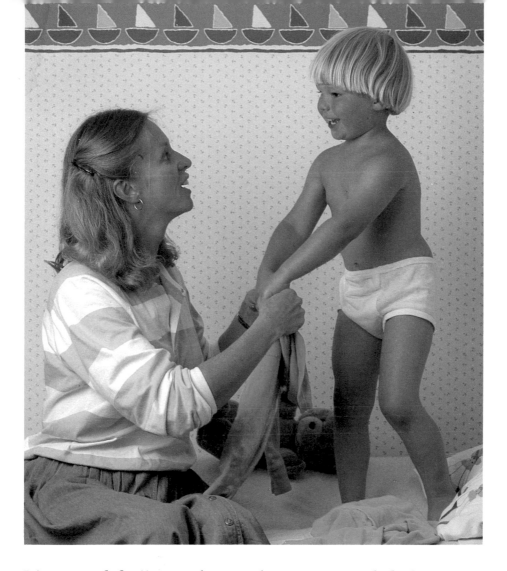

It's a good feeling to know that moms and dads like helping their children to grow! There's so much to learn while we're growing. And everyone needs help from time to time. But soon you may be wearing underpants and staying dry all day and all night, too!

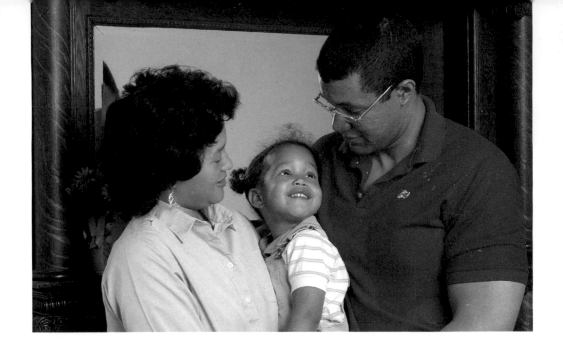

What's more, you'll have learned to do something new—
all by yourself. And you and the people who love you
best can be really proud of the way you're growing.